©BRIAN GLENN INNERVISIONS 2017 ALL RIGHTS RESERVED

EFT

EMOTIONAL FREEDOM TECHNIQUE

Brian Glenn

©BRIAN GLENN INNERVISIONS 2017 ALL RIGHTS RESERVED

CONTENTS

INTRODUCTION 4

DISCLAIMER 5

VIDEOS 6

EMOTIONAL FREEDOM TECHNIQUE 7

    THE DISCOVERY STATEMENT 8

SUD LEVEL 9

    USING THE EFT 11
    PROPER EFT TAPPING 11
    IT'S ALL IN THE FINGERTIPS 12

THE 'SORE' SPOT 14

THE SETUP PHRASE 14

    CHOOSING EFT'S SETUP PHRASES 15
    OTHER EFT PHRASE OPTIONS 16

THE TAPPING POINTS 18

    REMINDER PHRASE 19
    COGNITIVE SHIFTS (ASPECTS) 25
    USING EFT'S AFFIRMATION STATEMENTS 27

TECHNIQUES 34

    CHOICES TECHNIQUE 34
    THE MOVIE TECHNIQUE 40
    THE STORY TELLING TECHNIQUE 41
    PSYCHOLOGICAL REVERSALS 42

WHAT TO DO WHEN YOU ARE NOT GETTING RESULTS 45

CONDUCTING A CLIENT SESSION 47

EFT TELEPHONE SESSIONS 48

PSYCHOLOGICAL REVERSAL 54

    GENERAL POLARITY REVERSAL 54
    HOW TO CORRECT GENERAL POLARITY REVERSAL 56
    SECONDARY GAIN/ LOSS REVERSALS 56
    CRITERIA RELATED REVERSALS 58

INNERVISIONS SCHOOL OF CLINICAL HYPNOSIS 61

    ACCREDITATION 63

INTRODUCTION

Emotional Freedom Technique, or EFT, is the psychological acupressure technique I routinely use in my practice, and most highly recommend to optimise your emotional health. Although it is still often overlooked, emotional health is absolutely essential to your physical health and healing. No matter how devoted you are to the proper diet and lifestyle, you will not achieve your body's ideal healing and preventative powers if emotional barriers stand in your way.

You don't need to just use EFT to address specific things; you can also use it as a preventative measure, making EFT a regular part of your daily routine.

Use EFT daily on yourself, friends, family, and even animals! Children also love EFT, make it a fun part of their everyday routine.

Enjoy...

Brian Glenn.
PRINCIPAL
INNERVISIONS SCHOOL OF CLINICAL HYPNOSIS

DISCLAIMER

This book does not provide medical advice.

The content is for informational purposes only. Consult with your Doctor (GP) on all medical issues regarding your condition and its treatment.

The Content is not intended to be a substitute for professional medical advice, diagnosis, or treatment. It is not a substitute for a medical examination, nor does it replace the need for services provided by a medical professional.

Always seek the advice of your medical professional before making any changes to your treatment. Any medical questions should be directed to your personal doctor.

Brian Glenn (the book author) or Innervisions School of Clinical Hypnosis make no warranties, either expressed or implied concerning the accuracy, applicability, reliability or suitability of the contents of this book.

Brian Glenn (the book author) or Innervisions School of Clinical Hypnosis shall in no event be held liable for any direct, indirect incidental or other consequential damages arising directly or indirectly from any use of the information contained in this book.

All content is for information only and is not warranted for content accuracy or any other implied or explicit purpose.

VIDEOS

In order to maximise your learning experience, I have created a unique website containing video of EFT methodologies to accompany and compliment this book.

The website is password protected, and a password will be emailed to you on receipt of the online application form from the following website address.

www.innervisionsuk.com/eft

EMOTIONAL FREEDOM TECHNIQUE

EFT is very easy to learn, and will help you:

- Remove Negative Emotions
- Reduce Food Cravings
- Reduce or Eliminate Pain
- Implement Positive Goals

EFT is a form of psychological acupressure, based on the same energy meridians used in traditional acupuncture to treat physical and emotional ailments for over five thousand years, but without the invasiveness of needles. Instead, simple tapping with the fingertips is used to input kinetic energy onto specific meridians on the head and chest while you think about your specific problem - whether it is a traumatic event, addiction, pain, etc. -- and voice positive affirmations.

This combination of tapping the energy meridians and voicing positive affirmations works to clear the "short-circuit" - the emotional block -- from your body's bio energy system, thus restoring your mind and body's balance, which is essential for optimal health and the healing of physical disease.

Some people are initially wary of these principles that EFT is based on - the electromagnetic energy that flows through the body and regulates our health is only recently becoming recognised in the West. Others are initially taken aback by (and sometimes amused by) the EFT tapping and affirmation methodology, whose basics you will learn here.

But keep in mind that, more than any traditional or alternative method I have used or researched, EFT works. I have witnessed the results in my clients since deciding to use EFT in June of 2004. The pioneer of EFT, Gary Craig, has seen similar outstanding results since developing EFT over a decade ago (see his website at www.emofree.com). Indeed, because of its very high rate of success, the use of EFT has spread rapidly.

This manual will provide an overview on how and where to tap, and the proper affirmation techniques, so that you can begin using EFT immediately to help yourself and others.

THE DISCOVERY STATEMENT

"The cause of all negative emotions is a disruption in the body's energy system."

Negative emotions come about because you are tuned in to certain thoughts or circumstances, which in turn, cause your energy system to disrupt.

Otherwise, you function normally. One's fear of heights is not present, for example, while one is reading the comic section of the Sunday newspaper and therefore not tuned in to the problem.

Tuning in to a problem can be done by simply thinking about it.

Thinking about the problem will bring about the energy disruptions involved, which then and only then can be balanced by applying The Basic Recipe.

Without tuning in to the problem, thereby creating those energy disruptions, EFT does nothing.

SUD LEVEL

SUD is an acronym for 'subjective unit of discomfort' and refers to your client's level of emotional or physical pain. This will give you a logical indication of the strength of the negative emotions that they are presenting with.

For example, the client presenting with physical pain could be asked how bad the pain is on a level of zero to ten. (A level of zero would indicate 'no pain', and ten would indicate excruciating pain).

As a professional therapist, you must consider a safe and ethical level to reduce the SUD level. For example, a client with a SUD level of 10 who presents with a fear of heights would not be safe if you reduced it to zero.

It may be a good idea to discuss with your client an acceptable future SUD level and in some cases it could actually be a zero. (i.e. feelings of hatred toward someone)

Also, as much as your client wants that zero (consciously) the subconscious may only agree to a level that is acceptable to it! – Secondary gains could be too hard to get past.

It is always a good idea to ask your client what their SUD level is, in layman's terms, so that both you and your client are able to successfully monitor future progress.

"On a scale of zero to ten, what is the level of your discomfort regarding this issue? Where zero is no discomfort and 10 is maximum possible discomfort."

USING THE EFT

There are two basic areas to learn in order to use EFT:

1. The tapping locations and technique.
2. The positive affirmations.

These areas, as well as some advanced EFT principles and techniques, are covered in the following sections.

You should be able to successfully treat many problems by diligently applying the following instructions.

PROPER EFT TAPPING

The basic EFT sequence is straightforward and generally takes my clients only a few minutes to learn. They have the slight advantage of me personally showing them the tapping points, but you should be able to pick up these points relatively quickly. With a little practice, you will be performing each round in under a minute.

NOTE: While it is important to tap the correct area, you need not worry about being absolutely precise, as tapping the general area is sufficient.

IT'S ALL IN THE FINGERTIPS

The first thing to understand is that you will be tapping with your fingers. There are a number of acupuncture meridians on your fingertips, and when you tap with your fingertips, you are also likely using not only the meridians you are tapping on but also the ones on your fingers.

Traditional EFT has you tapping with the fingertips of your index finger and middle finger and with only one hand. Either hand works just as well. Most of the tapping points exist on either side of the body, so it doesn't matter which side you use, nor does it matter if you switch sides during the tapping. For example, you can tap under your right eye and, later in the tapping, under your left arm.

Ideally, you will want to use your fingertips, not your finger pads as they have more meridian points. However, if you are a woman with long fingernails you should of course, use your finger pads (otherwise you may end up stabbing yourself).

You should also remove your watch and bracelets, as that will interfere with your use of the wrist meridian tapping.

TAP SOLIDLY - BUT DON'T HURT YOURSELF!

You should tap solidly, but never so hard as to hurt or bruise yourself.

If you decide to use both hands, I recommend slightly alternating the tapping so that each hand is slightly out of phase with the other and you are not tapping with both hands simultaneously. This provides a kinaesthetic variant of the alternating eye movement work that is done in EMDR and may have some slight additional benefit.

When you tap on the points outlined below, you will tap about five to seven times. The actual number is not critical, but ideally should be about the length of time it takes for one full breath. There is probably a distinct benefit for tapping through one complete respiration cycle.

Please notice that these tapping points proceed down the body. That is, each tapping point is below the one before it. That should make it a snap to memorise. You can tap the points in any order and sequence, just so long as all the points are covered. It just is easier to go from top to bottom to make sure you remember to do them all.

REMOVE YOUR GLASSES AND WATCH PRIOR TO TAPPING

Glasses and watches can mechanically and electromagnetically interfere with EFT, so I advise everyone to remove them prior to tapping. For quick sessions conducted upon yourself, this is not critical, as you can easily tap around them, but I think there is always a benefit to removing them when possible.

THE 'SORE' SPOT

First, we need to locate our sore spot. It's a relatively tender place not far from your collarbone; if you press inwards with your fingers, you should be able to find it after spending a minute or so just 'prodding' around the area.

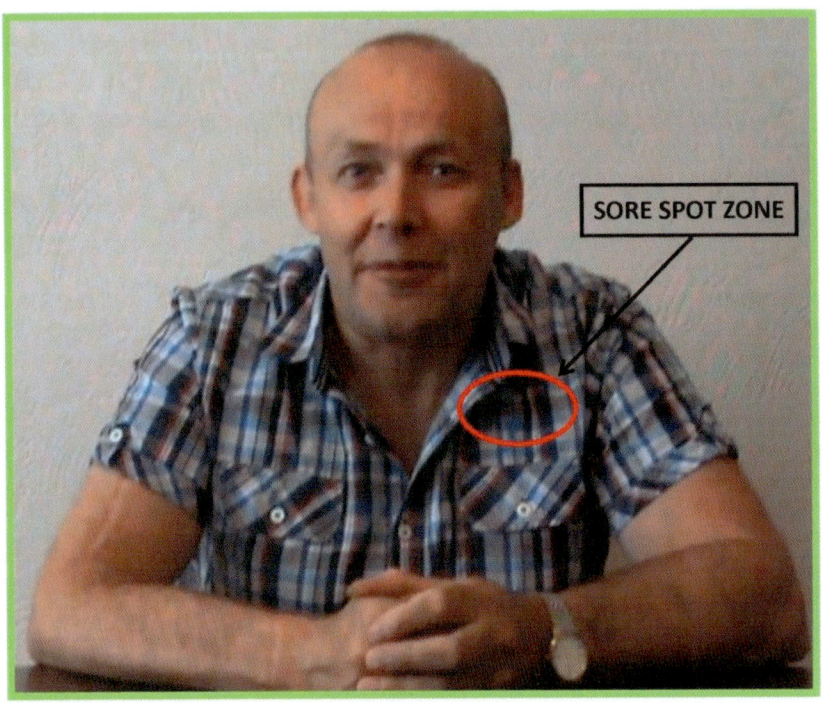

THE SETUP PHRASE

As you massage your 'sore spot', say your setup phrase out aloud three or four times with passion.

CHOOSING EFT'S SETUP PHRASES

TUNING INTO YOUR PROBLEM

The traditional EFT phrase uses the following setup:

"Even though I have this _____,

I deeply and completely accept myself."

You can also substitute this as the second part of the phrase:

"I deeply and completely love and accept myself."

The blank above is filled in with a brief description of the addiction, food craving, negative emotion or other problem you want to address.

EXAMPLES USING THE TRADITIONAL EFT PHRASING

While these examples represent a range of problems, keep in mind there really is no limit to the types of issues you can confront with EFT:

"Even though I have this fear of public speaking, I deeply and completely accept myself."

"Even though I have this headache, I deeply and completely accept myself."

"Even though I have this anger towards my father, I deeply and completely accept myself."

"Even though I have this war memory, I deeply and completely accept myself."

"Even though I have this stiffness in my neck, I deeply and completely accept myself."

"Even though I have these nightmares, I deeply and completely accept myself."

"Even though I have this craving for alcohol, I deeply and completely accept myself."

"Even though I have this fear of snakes, I deeply and completely accept myself."

"Even though I have this depression, I deeply and completely accept myself."

OTHER EFT PHRASE OPTIONS

You can also try these other phrase variations. All of these affirmations are correct because they follow the same general format. That is, they acknowledge the problem and create self-acceptance despite the existence of the problem. That is what's necessary for the affirmation to be effective.

You can use any of them, but I suggest you use the recommended one above because it is easy to memorise and has a good track record at getting the job done.

"I accept myself even though I have this_____."

Or:

"Even though I have this _____, I deeply and profoundly accept myself."

Or:

"I love and accept myself even though I have this_____."

Important Points About the Affirmation Statements

It doesn't matter whether you believe the affirmation or not...just say it.

It is better to say it with feeling and emphasis, but saying it routinely will usually do the job.

It is best to say it out loud, but if you are in a social situation where you prefer to mutter it under your breath... or do it silently... then go ahead. It will still likely be effective.

Use the client's language patterns (or yours when working on yourself).

Tuning in is seemingly a very simple process. You merely think about the problem while applying the tapping. That's it... at least in theory.

THE TAPPING POINTS

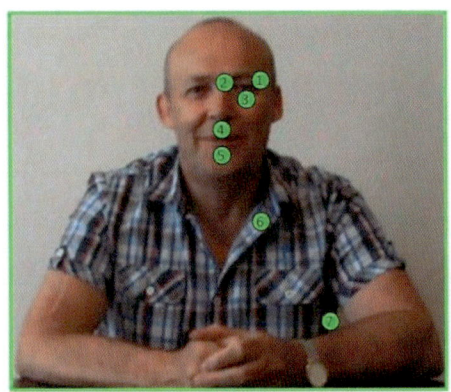

As you gently tap on the five area's on your face, one on your collarbone, and then one under your arm (where your bra strap is) you can sequentially move down to your hand and tap areas eight to thirteen.

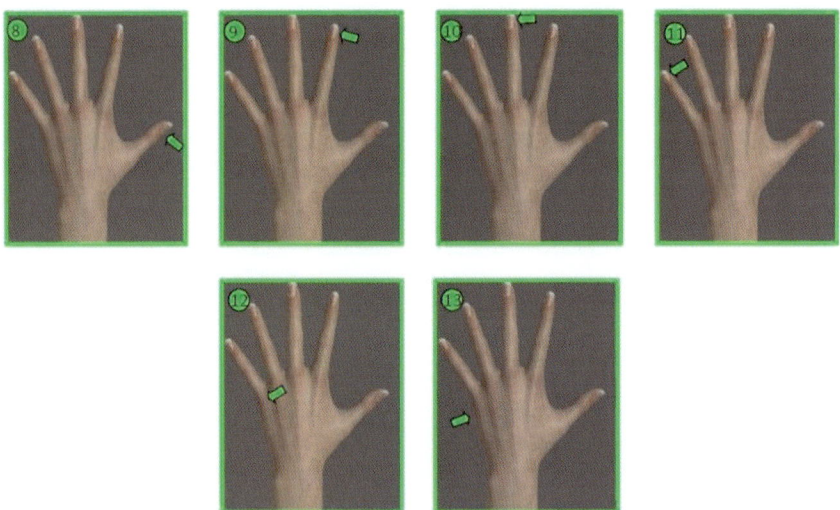

As you tap, remember to say out aloud a reminder phrase.

REMINDER PHRASE

Use your "reminder phrase" whilst doing a round of tapping. This is simply a word or short phrase that describes the problem and which you repeat out loud each time you tap one of the thirteen points in the sequence. In this way, you continually "remind" your energy system about the problem you are working on.

The best reminder phrase to use is usually identical to what you choose for the setup phrase you initially used. However, you can use a short cut if the setup is particularly long, by simply saying one or several words to speed up the process and do more rounds.

For example, if you are working on a fear of public speaking, the initial, or "setup," affirmation would go like this:

"Even though I have this fear of public speaking, I deeply and completely accept myself."

Within this affirmation, the underlined words "fear of public speaking" are ideal candidates for use as the reminder phrase.

Simply repeating this reminder phrase are usually sufficient to "tune in" to the problem at hand.

BRAINWAVE PROCEDURE

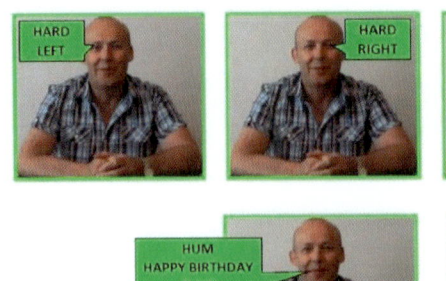

After the thirteen tapping points have been tapped and the appropriate phrases repeated, we finish off the sequence by doing the following brainwave procedure.

1. With head facing forward, move your eyes hard down to the left.

2. With head facing forward, move your eyes hard down to the right.

3. With head facing forward, roll your eyes in a circle clockwise.

4. With head facing forward, roll your eyes in a circle anti clockwise.

5. Hum happy birthday to you.

6. Count from one to five

The above sequence engages various brainwave patterns as the sequence continues. Humming 'happy birthday to you' engages the right brain (creative side) and counting from one to five engages the left brain (analytical side) Please note that the tune you hum does not have to be 'happy birthday to you', it's just that everyone knows that tune! You could actually hum your favourite tune instead if you choose to.

SUMMARY

So let's now put the whole EFT sequence together.

1. Ascertain appropriate sud level.

2. Devise an appropriate affirmation.

3. Carefully "tune in" to your problem by actually holding the problem in your thought.

4. State the affirmations in a loud voice with great passion, energy and enthusiasm while at the same time massaging your sore spot.

5. Tap gently on the thirteen tapping points while at the same time repeating out loud, your 'reminder statement.'

6. Finish off with your head forward and the brainwave procedure.

7. Got to item 4 in this list.

8. Repeat this sequence three times.

9. Check sud level.

10. Repeat if sud level is not down to a satisfactory level and adapt or change your setup phrase.

SUMMARY DIAGRAM

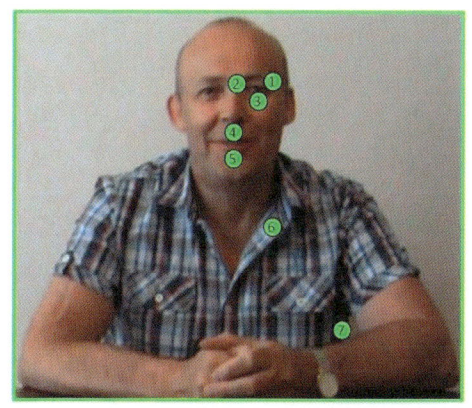

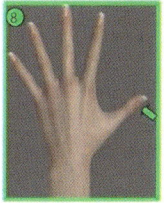 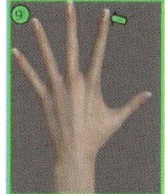 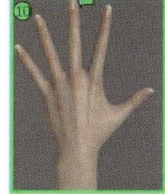 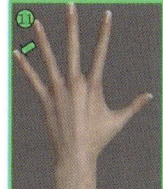

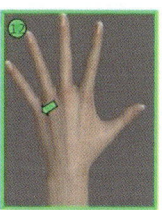 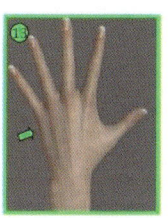

LINGERING ISSUES: ADJUSTMENTS FOR SUBSEQUENT ROUNDS OF TAPPING

Sometimes the first round of tapping doesn't completely eliminate a problem because new issues or issues that prevent further progress show themselves via the tapping.

These issues, whether images, conversations, interactions or in some other form, are in some way related to the first problem being addressed. Sometimes they are part of or the core of the cause; sometimes they are a result. The barrier restricting your emotional health, in other words, is made up of more than one brick and you must eliminate all the bricks.

If this is the case, you should do additional rounds of tapping, as necessary, to eliminate all the issues, but adjust your affirmation slightly, as follows, for best results:

"Even though I still have some of this _____, I deeply and completely accept myself."

Note the words "still" and "some" and how they change the thrust of the affirmation toward the remainder of the problem.

EFT CAUTIONS AND ADVICE

BE SPECIFIC

It is essential for clinicians to be extremely specific with language when using EFT.

TUNING IN

The clients need to be totally tuned in to the issue of concern when using EFT. Sometimes, when the material is emotionally painful, clients will want to disconnect from their feelings. Look for any signs that the client is becoming distracted or disengaged, and make sure that they repeat the Reminder Phrase as they tap the treatment points.

COGNITIVE SHIFTS (ASPECTS)

As with energy movement, it is essential to pay attention to the cognitive shifts that can occur with even a single round of the tapping. A cognitive shift has occurred when you reframe the problem. Seeing the problem from a new angle, you will often express a sense of surprise and insight.

These movements can offer valuable connections and associations and may open new pathways for healing. Following a cognitive shift, you often feel less guilt and self-blame, more hope, or a simple sense of relief in an area where there has never been relief before.

It is important to stop after tapping and see if you notice anything different, or if something new came up after you tapped. This is frequently the underlying issue that is the real root of your problem.

USE IT ON EVERYTHING

EFT can be used to treat deep limiting beliefs, fears of the future, fear of success, fear of failure, and anxiety about expectations, poor body image and future relapse settings. One of the favourite sayings of Gary Craig, founder of EFT, is "Try it on everything."

ENERGY AND INTENTION

Many clients report that they do not have the same success when using EFT by themselves and on themselves. This likely has to do, in part, with the advantage of combining the energy and intention of two people sharing a single purpose during a session. When clients are less than satisfied with their own results, it is best to find a therapist to help them resolve the issue at a deeper level.

THROUGH ME, NOT BY ME

This is one of Gary Craig's other favourite sayings. EFT practitioners are NOT healing their clients. The healing is done through us if our clients are open to receive it.

Many people see themselves as special healers. This, in fact, interferes with the treatment process. The reality is that they are not healing anybody; the clients are actually healing themselves. Witnessing and facilitating this process is humbling as well as gratifying.

KEEP WELL HYDRATED

Water conducts electricity, and EFT accesses the electrical energy that flows through our bodies and minds. It is very important for both you and your clients to be adequately hydrated. That would be about one quart of pure water per day for every fifty pounds of body weight.

USING EFT'S AFFIRMATION STATEMENTS

More On Your Affirmations

Doing affirmations is one of the best ways to be kind to your mind, every thought you have, every sentence you speak is an affirmation of a sort. It is either positive or negative. However, you can also do specific intentional affirmations. And the beautiful thing about doing affirmations is that you can radically improve the effectiveness with EFT.

You can do this by first creating a definite positive statement that builds you up instead of beats you up. We're talking about definite positive statements to make or do something in our lives or to create a specific goal.

You can start this process with positive self-statements. Even if it doesn't feel true to begin with, you will want to do these statements or affirmations many times a day.

TIMING OF YOUR AFFIRMATIONS

When you wake up, when you go to bed, every time you go to the bathroom you should say them.

It is especially important to tap and say the affirmations before you go to sleep. This is probably the single most important time to do it. I can't encourage you enough to do the EFT affirmations every night. It is one of the most important principles I can give you. When you tap before you go to bed you will give your subconscious from 6-8 hours to work on your affirmations and help create them for you.

It took me a nearly a year after learning EFT before I got in the habit of tapping before going to bed, but I want you to avoid my mistake and not wait awhile before you start doing this valuable technique. Start tapping each and every night before you go to bed.

MIRROR WORK

This is actually quite simple and inexpensive; all you need is a mirror and some time. You can certainly tap alone or in the dark, but I find it is far more effective to tap while staring at your own eyes in the mirror. This seems to provide a far deeper connection with your subconscious. It's almost as if the mirror is reflecting back your energy into you, rather than going out into space somewhere.

If you haven't tried this yet you really need to consider doing this profoundly simple yet powerful technique.

You can begin by looking in the mirror and doing your EFT affirmations and you can tap that in on all the EFT points. Pay careful attention and listen to what you hear, especially focusing on any negative messages that can be blocking your progress.

You may not get any messages initially because you are so used to beating yourself up and you are not used to a kind loving thought, but listen and follow through and learn to trust yourself.

We frequently have a tendency to beat ourselves up for every little thing no matter how small. All of us can use forgiveness on a daily basis and you can use the mirror to help you here also.

You can start by looking into your own eyes and say "Even though I wasn't successful or I was angry or mean or cruel or whatever problem you need to forgive yourself for then say "I forgive you, I was only doing the best I could".

"I forgive you for holding onto those patterns for too long, I forgive you for not loving yourself."

And when you say "you" you are looking directly into your own eyes.

You have to try this as it is quite powerful. Remember to always acknowledge the negative thought if it is there, but don't give it a lot of importance.

Then you will want to use EFT on the negative thought that comes up and create a positive opposite.

THE REAL REASON WHY YOU CAN'T ACHIEVE YOUR GOAL OR LOSE WEIGHT

A very common occurrence that will present itself is when you start to tap for a food craving you will have a memory of an image, person, place or event that the craving reminds you of. When you are doing the tapping sequences you will want to pay special attention to these usually negative thoughts or images that come up. Carefully listen for any statements that your subconscious is telling you are not right or true for you.

This is writing on your wall and causing a psycho energetic block, and unless you address that, reversal is not going to allow you to progress forward. This is usually the major challenge for you, and one of the primary reasons as to why you have not been able to successfully implement your goal in the past. Unless you directly address this issue by some means, it invariably will self-sabotage your efforts to achieve your weight loss goal.

Fortunately the solution is quite straightforward with EFT, you simply acknowledge whatever self-critical thoughts, images or feelings come up and then chose to simply love and accept yourself, while tapping on your acupuncture meridians.

Do this persistently, and eventually your system will improve with time. Remember to say your statements with great enthusiasm and all the emotions you can muster. Your subconscious mind will not convert your affirmations into reality unless you can tie the statements in with emotional energy.

Let me provide a few examples to illustrate my point more fully. When I once gave an EFT demonstration in front of 40 clinical nutritionists, I had a volunteer come up who had a food craving. It turns out the physician who volunteered had a craving for rice crispy treats that were in the exhibit area. Her craving was a strong 10. As soon as we did one round of tapping, her eyes started to water, and she was on the verge of tears. When I explored the issue further with her, she said that she was reminded of the time when her mother would give her M & M treats to get her out of her hair.

So the real issue had nothing to do with her craving for the treats, but it was the love and attention that her mother did not give her, and the clearly inferior sweetie substitute that her mother offered her. We tapped on that issue and her cravings for the sweets disappeared instantly.

Another example would be a woman I saw who was 64 years old and was having trouble losing weight. When we started the EFT affirmation sequence she had a memory of how the last time she was her normal goal weight, she was pregnant. Even though consciously she very well knew that short of a miracle she was not going to become pregnant at 64; she was blocked from going forward with her weight loss. Her subconscious was convinced that if she achieved her goal weight she would instantly and immediately become pregnant.

Fortunately, we were able to use EFT to bridge the gap to the subconscious and connect it back to reality. Once we completed tapping that issue through she was able to successfully lose the 22 pounds of weight she had been unable to do for over 20 years.

This is a very powerful illustration that the subconscious is absolutely neutral. Remember your subconscious is your faithful servant and it will provide you with exactly what you tell it. It couldn't care less whatever demand you place on it. In many ways it is like your computer. It will perform whatever instructions you tell it. So you must be very careful of the instructions you provide.

The above story illustrates a negative example of the power of the subconscious, but you could just as easily implant positive affirmations, and your subconscious will just as reliably provide you with that result in your life. I offer some practical suggestions on how to take advantage of this principle below.

BE PERSISTENT WITH YOUR AFFIRMATIONS

When you first say an affirmation it may not seem to be true. Please remember that affirmations are like planting seeds in the ground. It helps if you think of our mind like a garden in which your thoughts are seeds that you are planting. When you do these affirmations it is like putting a new seed into the ground.

Remember when you plant a seed in the ground, you only have a little tiny seed, you don't have a full-grown plant. That little seed needs to germinate. Then it breaks open its little shell and it starts to get nourishment from the earth. Then first the roots come out, and then and only then, does that first little shoot come out through the ground.

Just like it takes some time to go from seed to a full-grown plant, it takes some time from your first affirmation to the realisation of your goal. It doesn't matter whether you see the results or you don't see them. You have to trust that it just takes time.

BE PATIENT WITH YOUR AFFIRMATIONS

A critical truth that is helpful to remember when doing this work is that your persistent and consistent thoughts will eventually become your reality, so be careful to only focus on positive thoughts.

So many people do EFT affirmations for a few days, they say it doesn't work, and they stop. Remember, everything happens in a perfect time space sequence. You want to trust that and we want to know that.

Fortunately, EFT seems to rapidly accelerate not only the time at which your goal is realised but the likelihood for your success. From my experience, it is one of the most profoundly effective ways to maximise the success of your affirmations.

BE PRESENT WITH YOUR AFFIRMATIONS

Be sure to always remember to say your positive statements in the present tense. Your subconscious mind is very literal and if you ask it to do something in the future, you may fail to achieve your goal. So many of us commonly default to this by force of habit. It takes quite a bit of conscious effort to avoid this non-intentional self-defeating trap. So always avoid saying I will have or I am going to have, which is in the future tense.

Always say your affirmation in the present tense; otherwise you run the serious risk delay your obtaining what you want and you may never get it.

TECHNIQUES

CHOICES TECHNIQUE

Identify the negative emotion or state (thought, attitude, feeling, pain, etc.) that you want to be rid of.

Formulate a Choice that is roughly the opposite of this negative emotion or state.

Combine the negative emotion with the positive Choice.

State the entire Basic recipe combination (negative emotion and Choice).

Then alternate the points by stating the negative reminder phrase on one point and then the positive Choice or reminder Choice on the next point.

Be careful to always end on a positive Choice.

WORDING OF CHOICES

Most people do not know how to identify what they really want. Ironically, however, they are almost always very clear about what they don't want.

When asked to make a positive Choice, which is based on what they do want, most people will at best, just choose to improve a bit on what they don't like. One way they do this is to revert to comparisons.

They will use such words as better or more.

Examples include:

- I choose to be more confident.
- I choose to feel better.

This does not work well because a person's subconscious, computer-like mind is quite literal and it cannot interpret that statement with any precision. What is better? It could be only a tiny bit better. How much is more? When this is not spelled out precisely you have an unclear Choice that will not be very effective.

FIRST RULE OF CHOICES: BE SPECIFIC

A person making a Choice needs to state precisely what it is they want. A Choice should not contain vague comparison words such as "better," but should be a statement of exactly what they really want to create in their life.

SECOND RULE OF CHOICES: CREATE A PULLING CHOICE (SELL BENEFITS)

Choices must "pull" to be effective. This requirement is often neglected. A Choice that is lifeless is like a dull ad; you just skip over it, don't attend to it, and it has very little impact on your life.

You might think of a choice as a sort of ad made up by you and directed to yourself as a consumer. The person who must be sold is you. You have to buy into and truly want the manifestation you are trying to bring about.

Whenever possible seek to carefully add an adjective or adjectives to make the Choice as appealing as possible. The aim is to draw you like a magnet toward the goal they seek. Repeating the Choice during the EFT session should be a source of real pleasure and comfort, so that you really want to keep saying the Choice over and over, simply because it is so enjoyable to do so.

Examples:

- Let it be easy to...
- Surprise myself by...
- Find a creative way to...
- Find it fun to...

Alternatively you can add any of these adjectives to give it more appeal:

- Comfortable
- Satisfying
- Delightful
- Ingenious
- Safe
- Unexpected

THIRD RULE OF CHOICES: GO FOR THE BEST POSSIBLE OUTCOME

The rule of thumb here is to be inwardly "truthful" in what is asked for. You need to choose what you really want in your innermost self, not what you think you should want - and it should be the very best you can imagine having.

EXAMPLES:

It is not enough to choose to have a "new apartment," because a "new apartment" might be a dingy 6th story walk-up with poor heating, tiny rooms, etc. Yet technically it might be "new" for you. A much more effective Choice would be to state exactly what you really want, such as "I choose to live in a quiet, sunny, delightful apartment".

The more positive and specific you are the better the Choice will be.

Fourth Rule of Choices: State Your Choice in the Positive

Those who have worked with affirmations know that the literalness of the computer-mind makes negative words or phrases a large problem. Our mind tends to ignore the negative and we get exactly what we were hoping to avoid.

We are always better off being as positive as we can when framing any sort of command to ourselves - and affirmations are basically commands.

When making a choice, therefore you should avoid using such negative words and phrases as:

- No
- Not
- Never
- Don't
- Be Rid of

For Example:

- Poor Way: I want to be rid of my headache.
- Better Way: I choose to feel clear-headed, healthy, focused and enthusiastic.

FIFTH RULE OF CHOICES: DO NOT CHOOSE FOR OTHERS

This rule is important to emphasise because some people will choose other's behaviour as though they had control over other people, which none of us have.

For Example:

- I choose to have Mary love me.
- I choose to have the people at work think I'm the best.
- I choose to have Ken understand me.

There are many ways that the above incorrectly worded Choices can be reworded so as to be non-manipulative and ethical in nature.

Preferred:

I choose to feel that Mary loves me. Here the person is making a Choice about their own reaction to Mary, something quite within their control.

The details are less important than the intent when applying this rule. The point here is not to act as though we were all-powerful in another person's life, but rather word the Choice so as to be as genuinely helpful to them as possible without imposing your values on them.

THE MOVIE TECHNIQUE

The movie technique is a tool that is used to identify more specific events rather than global issues. If we work with global issues then we may not get the results we desire.

MOVIE TECHNIQUE PROTOCOL

The movie has a specific beginning and end with a plot and characters. An example of a global problem would be "my mother ".

If the client makes a movie of "my mother stresses me out", then the client will refer to a specific event.

Ask the client if the issue was a movie, how long would the movie last? If the client tells you that the movie would last hours, then the client isn't giving you a specific event.

If you ask the client to give their movie a title, then this will make them identify a specific event. The title could be…?

Ask them to make the mental movie in their mind and ask what is the intensity as they think about the event. If dealing with an extremely emotional issue/trauma/phobia then do not ask them to make a mental movie of the issue, tap on the title of the movie only, "this _____ issue" and ask them to guess what they think that the intensity might be.
When tapping use "this _____ movie". Check intensity after each round of tapping. When the intensity is at a zero,

ask the client to run through the movie in their mind again and if they feel any intensity to stop at that point.

Emphasize to your client that they must stop when they feel the intensity, so that further tapping can be done to eliminate the identified feeling/aspect. Tap on the feeling until it is reduced to zero intensity.

Ask the client to re-run the movie from start to finish, tap on feelings as they come up. Keep re-running the movie from start to finish until there is no intensity left in the movie.

To check that the charge has gone, ask them to imagine this movie one more time, but ask them to turn up the colours, sounds, bring the picture closer to them, and try to get themselves upset about it. If the client does find some intensity, tap until the intensity is gone and then repeat this exercise.

THE STORY TELLING TECHNIQUE

This technique has the client verbalise the story. The client narrates the story about the specific event, stopping when they reach intense parts of the story. Firstly, ask the client how they feel about the thought of telling the story.
Again ask the client to identify a specific event and tell the story to you. When the client comes to an emotionally tense part they are to stop and tap on that intensity. Again inform the client of the importance of this. (May miss chance to heal if they do not so). Ask them to tell the story again, stopping to tap if necessary. Repeat this process until

there is no charge left in the story. This technique helps to identify aspects of the problem.

To test - ask the client to imagine the scene from start to finish, turning up the colours, sounds etc., ask them to try to get upset about it. If intensity is found, tap on the aspect and then re-test.

Unlike the traditional affirmations mentioned above, Choices do not contradict a person's present view of reality and so are much more easily accepted. Additionally, the represent a proactive stance and a commitment to one's self.

When using the Choices option a self-acceptance affirmation is substituted for the traditional EFT affirmation used above. In general, this affirmation is the opposite of whatever the negative statement contained in the first portion of the Set-Up phrase.

This Choice is an expression of what the person truly desires for the problem that the treatment is presently addressing. It is aimed at that specific problem rather than being a general affirmation.

PSYCHOLOGICAL REVERSALS

Unconscious resistance (to positive change), sabotaging yourself because of an inner conflict. Limiting belief(s) is causing stagnation.

Secondary gain, secondary benefit, therapy resistance. When you try really hard to accomplish therapy goals, it can be very painful to notice that part of you is actually sabotaging the process. You are fighting against yourself.

The most common reason that psychological reversal does not change is that the affirmation was not said strongly enough or with enough emphasis. Most people will quietly state the affirmation I have frequently seen that it was necessary for the client to nearly shout the statements prior to the reversal shifting.

CRITERIA RELATED REVERSALS

These are subconscious mechanisms that may be in place and blocking the client's ability to successfully resolve their reversal.

DESERVEDNESS

This is the most commonly seen of the criteria-related reversals. Common sense dictates that if a person consciously or unconsciously holds the position that he or she does not deserve to get over a problem, attempts to alleviate the problem will be met with considerable resistance. This reversal is common among trauma survivor, clients, with eating disorders, and those who have violated closely help personal values and morals.

SAFETY

If the client experiences the problem as affording some level of safety, it will not easily be resolved. This consideration does not necessarily apply to situations that are truly unsafe or dangerous. This reversal is common among clients with anxiety-related conditions and even clients suffering from chronic pain.

POSSIBILITY / DOUBT

Some clients experience deep doubt about their ability to resolve the presenting problem, for whatever reasons. While doubt by itself does not signal a reversal, if it is deep enough it will be consistent with a reversal.

PERMISSION

In many instances this operates in conjunction with another, such as safety or deservedness. It is as if the energy system is saying, "I won't allow myself to get over this problem because it isn't safe to get over it" or "I won't allow myself to overcome this problem because I don't deserve to get over it."

DEPRIVATION

Especially in the treatment of addictions, the issue of deprivation may serve to block progress. When this type of reversal is diagnosed, a discussion around this issue is appropriate.

WHAT TO DO WHEN YOU ARE NOT GETTING RESULTS

Negative beliefs may interfere with EFT or any energy treatment from working very effectively.

Some of the more common ones that might need to be treated include:

- I don't believe these treatments will work.

- I believe EFT works, but not for me.
- I doubt that EFT will work.
- Even if EFT does work, I am afraid it won't last.
- I don't trust myself to stay free of these problems from now on.
- I am afraid that these treatments won't work.
- I am afraid that the problem will come back.
- Here are common dynamics that show up as treatable problems. One needs to be alert to these.
- I'm afraid to give up my hopelessness, helplessness, fear, dependency, etc.
- I doubt it will happen.
- I'm supposed to be rejected.
- I don't trust myself to live it out.
- I'm supposed to be disapproved of.
- I don't feel safe with… (whatever the situation is)
- I have to be perfect about everything.
- I fear something like this problem will happen again.
- I doubt that I will really be able to do this.

CONDUCTING A CLIENT SESSION

1. Create rapport with client.
2. Gain some background of issue.
3. Explain to client what EFT is.
4. Inform the client of the benefits of using EFT (self-help tool, possible to achieve quicker results than some of the other therapies, how it will be beneficial to the client.
5. Inform to take responsibility for using techniques, does not replace any advice given by doctor.
6. Show client the routine and ask them to tap along.
7. Record SUD'S level (intensity of problem).
8. Be specific - work with a specific event or specific statement.
9. Tap with client (power of intention).
10. At the end of the round, ask client to take a deep breath in (this rebalances the energy).
11. Re assess SUD's level.
12. Check that the client is measuring the same issue rather than switching goal posts.
13. Proceed with further rounds.
14. Any intensity found then tap.
15. Re-test.
16. End of session - review session.
17. Ask Client how they found EFT.
18. Establish what still needs working on and arrange further session if necessary.

EFT TELEPHONE SESSIONS

Benefits

- Attract more customers and increase your business
- Client can have therapy in the comfort of their own home
- Clients saves time on travelling
- Preparation before the session

PRE-TALK

Inform the client the benefits of using EFT for them.

Explain to the client the EFT process. Inform client how it has been used to help other people.

You can either send the client a sheet with the tapping points on it, by e-mail or through the post or it is possible to talk the client through the tapping points. If the client is needing to use EFT at home during the sessions, then it is better if they have a sheet as a reminder of the points.

Ask the client if they have a room they can use during the session that they will not be disturbed. Reassure the client that the call will be confidential.

Ensure that you receive payment from the client before the session. Arrange how payment is to be made, and agree who is going to pay for the call. Build rapport with the client.

DURING THE SESSION

First round, explain where the tapping points are and tap with them, check if tapping the correct spot. Listen to the client's voice, this will give you clues to how well things are going. Listen to the tone of voice and the words they use. Does the client sound more relaxed or does the client sound tense or uptight? The practitioner can gain rapport with the client over the telephone by using expression or words.

If the client goes silent, ask them what is happening, what are they feeling or thinking? If you don't ask them then, the client may miss an opportunity for healing.

END OF SESSION

Identify what still needs working on and arrange another session. Ask the client how they found EFT.

HOW TO USE EFT WHEN OUT IN PUBLIC PLACES

(Can also be used by clients who do not feel comfortable doing the usual EFT when family are around).

MASSAGING THE POINTS

Instead of tapping, massage the points with one finger in a circular motion. This is a more inconspicuous way of doing EFT.

FINGER POINT ROUTINES

Tapping on the finger points is a good method to use when out in a public place. Here are two alternatives.

Use the thumb of the same hand to tap/massage the finger points of that hand. To be more discreet cover the hand you are working on with your other hand.

You can also tap/massage both hands at the same time. Again, use the thumb of the same hand to tap/massage the finger points of that hand. If sitting at a table, then placing hands under the table to tap/massage the points will be more discreet.

SINGLE POINT ROUTINE

After you have been using the EFT technique for a while, it is possible that a point may be identified which produces a shift for you. Instead of completing a full round of the EFT sequence, tap or massage continuously on the identified point. (Be careful not to tap or massage any single point too vigorously. Finding a single tapping point is also beneficial for individuals who are dealing with addiction. This single tapping point can be used as an emergency stop. This method of tapping will help reduce the intensity of the craving and may stop you giving in to the craving. An additional EFT routine may be necessary to reduce the intensity of the craving further.

TOUCH AND BREATHE METHOD

This method was developed by John Diepold and uses the same EFT sequence, but instead of tapping the points, lightly touch each point, whilst taking one breath in and out. Touch the points long enough to repeat your chosen reminder phrase. Use the same number of fingers that you would use in a tapping routine. The reminder phrase can be mentally said in your mind, instead of verbalising the phrase.

THE IMAGINATION METHOD

Visualise tapping on each point and instead of verbalising the EFT statement and phrase, mentally say the phrase in your mind. This method can be just as effective as the normal EFT routine. You may need to practice this before using this method when out in a public situation.

Some individuals find visualisation difficult. For such individuals, I suggest physically tapping or massaging the points while repeating the statement and chosen phrase in the mind.

THE KARATE CHOP POINT

If using the karate chop point for the set-up phrase or during a sequence, this point can be tapped while the hands are hidden underneath a table. If there is no table, then you can tap the karate chop point by tapping the side of your hand on to your leg.

TAPPING BEFORE THE EVENT

The EFT tapping technique can be used to prepare you before a situation happens. You will need to imagine the future situation and establish a level of intensity, then tap. This method is particularly beneficial for clients dealing with addictions. Tapping before the event helps to break association with the addiction in that event.

After tapping on the event, I also suggest using visualisation techniques to rehearse things going well during the event. Visualisation allows you to run through a future event in your mind. By using this technique you are able to rehearse coping well in that situation. It is important to repeat the visualisation several times, as the more the situation is visualised, the subconscious mind will accept the images as reality.

SHORT SEQUENCE ROUTINE

After using EFT for some time, you may be able to identify which points that shifts occur. The points identified can be used as a short cut version of the sequence. The points can be tapped or massaged, whichever is preferred.

If you are not able to identify any particular points, then using the under eye point and collarbone point are good options. An EFT Practitioner who has intuition skills may be able to identify points that may work well for the client.

I also suggest tapping on the additional points, top of the head (crown), the wrist points and ankle points is another option. The ankle points must not be used by pregnant women. These additional points were introduced to EFT by the Acupuncturist Michael Gandy and address 13 of the 14 meridians.

TAPPING IN A PRIVATE PLACE

Sometimes it may be possible to use the usual EFT technique if a private enough place can be found. If time is a factor, then a short sequence routine can be used.

PSYCHOLOGICAL REVERSAL

When Psychological Reversal is present, it blocks the EFT process from working. Negative thinking is a cause of Psychological Reversal. A more a person thinks negatively the more prone to PR they will be. Clients that are negative about everything are classed as being massively reversed. PR is usually present 40% of the time. For most issues PR may or may not be present in clients' issues. One client coming for treatment for anxiety may suffer from PR, but a client coming for the same issue, PR may not be present. PR will usually block progress in depression, addictions and degenerative disease cases. When weight loss clients relapse and self-sabotage themselves, this is because PR is present. There are different types of Psychological Reversal that stop the healing process.

GENERAL POLARITY REVERSAL

General Polarity Reversal is when the energy system is flowing in the wrong direction (reversed). Shock, trauma and fear can cause the energy flow to become reversed. If you imagine that the energy system works the same way as batteries. If the batteries are placed the wrong way round in an electrical item, then the item would simply not work. If the body's energy system is flowing in the wrong direction this will block EFT from working.

Have you ever had days where you were clumsy, stumbling over words, or had off days? This is probably because psychological reversal is in action.

It is not possible to tell if somebody's energy system is flowing in the wrong direction. A good clue to whether or not someone has GPR is if their SUDs (subjective unit of distress, scale of 1 to 10) remains the same, then they may very well be reversed.

HOW TO CORRECT GENERAL POLARITY REVERSAL

EFT has a built in system to overcome this energy flow problem. By applying the set-up, rubbing on the sore spot or tapping on the karate spot point and saying the set-up phrase will usually take care of this type of psychological reversal. Occasionally it might be necessary to rub the sore spot or tap the karate spot a little harder and say the set-up phrase with more emphasis to remove the PR. By performing the set-up it will ensure that the energy system is working correctly before the basic routine is applied.

Other factors that affect the energy flow are dehydration, energy toxins, food sensitivities and metals.

Dehydration - since the body's electrical system is conducted by water, the lack of water will cause the energy system to be sluggish or severely repressed.

Toxin or substance sensitivity - this could be something the subject just ate, clothing, carpeting, metal in or on the body; such as pins, fillings, metal plates, or even jewellery, a watch or a mobile phone.

Addictions - addictive personalities or addictive substances in the body (including alcohol, nicotine, drugs and sometimes medications).

SECONDARY GAIN/ LOSS REVERSALS

When the desired results are not being achieved, this may be because there may be some benefit/reason to keeping the problem. The individual may have the intention of getting over the problem but may have some reason why it might benefit them to keep the problem. Maybe a benefit of being overweight is that the individual will not have to spend money on new clothes. Or perhaps, someone trying to lose weight may feel that they will lose something if they give up overeating.

Secondary gain/loss issues must be tapped on in order for the individual to completely overcome the problem. If secondary gain/loss reversals are not eliminated then an individual trying to lose weight may find themselves self-sabotaging their efforts. When this happens this is not because of lack of willpower, but because this type of PR is present. By using muscle testing as a tool, this can establish what subconsciously are the client's intentions. Muscle testing can also be a diagnostic tool where the problem might reside.

In a client that wishes to lose weight, a secondary gain may be, they don't have to spend money on new clothes (Benefit of keeping the problem).

If little or no progress is being made, then asking questions around what is the benefit to keeping the problem? What is the downside to giving up the problem? Are there any self-limiting beliefs? What are the fears? May identify areas to work on.

E.g. of self-limiting belief - Never lose weight anyway as all my family are overweight.

Fears - new identity, how will people react to this new slender person (may not always be positive).

CRITERIA RELATED REVERSALS

Criteria Related reversals were introduced to EFT by Dr Fred Gallo. These type of reversals are subconscious and block the ability to heal.

Some individuals consciously or subconsciously believe that they do not deserve to get over the problem. This type of reversal is common in individuals with eating disorders and trauma survivors. To clear the reversal, tap on the statement "Even though I don't deserve to get over this problem", and identify any issues with this statement.

Individuals who have been suffering with a long term issue may feel that the issue is part of their life. This issue may have become part of their identify. In these cases, the subconscious mind may be reluctant to let go of this problem. Tap on statements such as "Even if I don't get over this problem" and "Even though I have fears of letting go of this problem" and identify any issues around these statements.

Issues around safety can also cause blocks. To clear the reversal tap on the statements "Even though it's unsafe for me to get over this problem" and "Even though it may be unsafe for others if I get over this problem" and identify any reasons for concern.

Some individuals doubt that they will get over the problem. Tap on the statement "Even if I don't get over this problem, I deeply and completely accept myself. What are the reasons for doubting? Tap on the reasons identified.

Deprivation can be another issue and is commonly found in individuals who have addictions and individuals trying to lose weight. The statement "Even though I will feel deprived without _____, I deeply and completely accept myself" can be used to remove the Psychological Reversal.

WILLPOWER

If an individual tries to overcome PR through willpower then they will find it an impossible task. Using willpower on a continuous basis drains the body of vast amounts of energy, and this can have an effect on the long term health of the individual. The inner conflict that goes on can express itself in physical disease, or mentally or psychologically. If the individual has other demands on them, such as being in a stress state, has depression or feeling generally run down, then it is likely that the willpower will collapse and the reverse parts will take over. Over a long term period, this can have an effect on a person's self-esteem and they consider themselves as weak. They are not weak, they just have PR present.

SHIFTING ASPECTS

Complex issues will have many other issues (aspects) that make up the problem. Often these aspects are other emotions. Sometimes a client may not notice an underlying issue until a more painful core issue has been reduced or eliminated. The hidden aspect can be the core issue. If other aspects are discovered whilst working on an issue, it is often better to bring down the original issue down to zero before working on other aspects. However, if the aspects are related to the original issue it is necessary to alleviate the shifting aspects before the original aspect will fall. (Use your own judgement).

INNERVISIONS SCHOOL OF CLINICAL HYPNOSIS

Established in 1996, Innervisions School of Clinical Hypnosis is the training provider of choice providing specialised training in modern clinical hypnosis. And with 21 years of training experience behind us, we are now one of the UK's leading training providers.

We aim to be the best in our particular field and to surpass our student's expectations; our teaching methods are unique, supportive, warm and friendly. We are dedicated to this profession and we intend to assist and train each and every student to become a competent practitioner in modern clinical hypnosis and hypnotherapy.

The course is designed to be of particular relevance to those in the caring profession as well as anyone who has an interest in the field of human potential and personal development. Whilst academic qualifications may be an advantage; we regard it as only being a small part of the learning curve to becoming a competent clinical hypnotherapist. This hypnotherapy training course is therefore open to those with a genuine interest in hypnotherapy irrespective of race, religion, and environmental classification, even though they may not have any relevant prior learning or training.

A UNIQUE OPPORTUNITY TO TRAIN FOR A REWARDING NEW CAREER

For two exciting days, Discover Hypnotherapy with our world class tutors and find out if hypnotherapy is the right career for you. You are invited to apply for a FREE place on our foundation weekend. Absolutely 100% free and unconditional.

www.innervisionsuk.com

ACCREDITATION

Our practitioner level training course has been assessed and validated at practitioner level by The General Hypnotherapy Standards Council (UK). Graduates are eligible for professional registration with The General Hypnotherapy Register at full practitioner status.

The GHSC was a key participant within the Working Group for Hypnotherapy Regulation whose primary purpose was to facilitate agreed standards within the profession and to subsequently bring about Voluntary Self-regulation (VSR), an officially recognised status, for the entire industry. To facilitate this, the Group actively co-operated with other industry representatives within the Hypnotherapy Regulatory Forum (a body established by the now defunct Prince's Foundation for Integrated Health) and as a consequence VSR was finally established via the Natural Healthcare Council (CNHC) set up in 2008 with Department of Health funding - when it admitted Hypnotherapy into its regulatory system on 1st December 2010.

DIPLOMA

Our Diploma in Hypnotherapy & Psychotherapy has been validated by the General Hypnotherapy Standards Council (GHSC) and Graduates from this course are eligible for professional registration with the General Hypnotherapy Register (the GHSC's registering agency) at full Practitioner status, together with the acquisition of the industry based award - the General Qualification in Hypnotherapy Practice (GQHP).

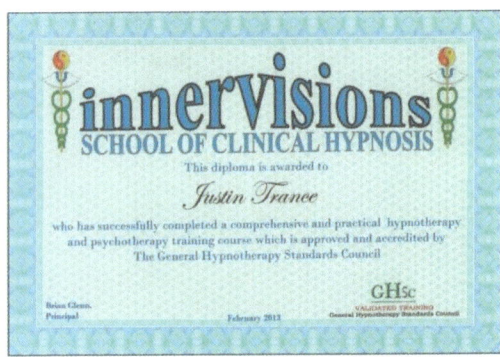

Graduates of this course will also be eligible to register with the Complementary & Natural Healthcare Council (CNHC). For more information visit **www.cnhc.org.uk**

For two exciting days, Discover Hypnotherapy with our world class tutors and find out if hypnotherapy is the right career for you. You are invited to apply for a FREE place on our foundation weekend. Absolutely 100% free and unconditional.

www.innervisionsuk.com

Printed in Great Britain
by Amazon